DYING CITY

BY CHRISTOPHER SHINN

★

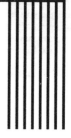

★

DRAMATISTS
PLAY SERVICE
INC.

DYING CITY
Copyright © 2007, Christopher Shinn

All Rights Reserved

DYING CITY was first presented by The English Stage Company
at the Royal Court Theatre, London.

Originally produced by Lincoln Center Theater,
New York City, 2007.

For E & L

DYING CITY was produced by Lincoln Center Theater in New York City on March 4, 2007. It was directed by James Macdonald; the set and costume design were by Anthony Ward; the lighting design was by Pat Collins; and the sound design was by Aural Fixation. The cast was as follows:

KELLY .... Rebecca Brooksher
CRAIG/PETER .... Pablo Schreiber

CHARACTERS

KELLY, late 20s
CRAIG, late 20s
PETER, late 20s

Craig and Peter are identical twins and played by the same actor.

SETTING

The play takes place in January 2004 and July 2005.

No interval; blackouts should be avoided; sound between scenes should not be over-designed. The play takes place in Kelly's apartment. A combined living room and kitchen is visible; doors lead to a bathroom and bedroom off. I imagined design that lives in naturalism but suggests something beyond it. I've kept stage directions to a minimum, omitting obvious actions, in an attempt to avoid clutter.

SETTING

The play takes place in January 2004 and June 2005.

"A lie sweet in the mouth is sour in the stomach."
—Aeschylus, *The Oresteia,*
translated by Ted Hughes

DYING CITY

1.

Night. Kelly sorts through books. A cardboard box sits next to the couch. TV plays Law & Order. *A bed sheet and pillow are scrunched up in the corner of the couch. The buzzer buzzes.*

KELLY. Hello?

PETER'S VOICE. Hi — it's Peter! *(Pause.)*

KELLY. Hi!

PETER'S VOICE. I tried calling ... *(Pause.)*

KELLY. Come up! *(Pause. Kelly throws the bed sheet over the box. Peter knocks.)* Hi! Peter ...

PETER. Hi Kelly — sorry!

KELLY. — Come in.

PETER. You're unlisted now!

KELLY. I am ...

PETER. I tried calling your land line, and then I tried your cell — I was wondering, I thought maybe it was a *work* thing, maybe one of your clients got your numbers or something and you/had to change —

KELLY. It's — yeah, it's. — I've been meaning to call you and — it's — I just haven't. I've been so/busy —

PETER. Oh, no, of course —

KELLY. I wanted to make sure I had the, that I had enough — energy, mental space, before I called ...

PETER. Did you, I wasn't — did you get my letter?

KELLY. — I did.

PETER. I was wondering, I wasn't sure if I had the right address —

KELLY. I did. Yeah, and I just — I've been *meaning* to call —

PETER. No — of *course.*

KELLY. So … *(Pause.)* Well — sit down, please! I'll make some tea.

PETER. Oh, tea would be lovely.

KELLY. Were you — in the neighborhood or — you're in town visiting…?

PETER. — I know, barging in like this, I have to apologize.

KELLY. Well — I don't have a phone.

PETER. *(Laughs.)* Right. No, I didn't plan on — tonight — it's actually a bit of a *drama* actually.

KELLY. Oh? *(Pause.)*

PETER. I'm sorry, is everything — did I, is it a bad — a bad/time or —

KELLY. No. No.

PETER. I just … *(Pause.)*

KELLY. You know, honestly — when they come to tell you — *(Pause.)* When they came to tell me about Craig, they just showed up — they just/show up, no warning, they don't call or —

PETER. Oh God. Oh Kelly, I'm so sorry. I'm so *stupid.*

KELLY. So I was just — a memory …

PETER. Of *course.*

KELLY. … of the buzzer — I'm fine.

PETER. God, I'm a total idiot.

KELLY. I'm fine.

PETER. And it's just about a year, right?

KELLY. Last week. Yeah.

PETER. Last *week.* Huh. I've been — the date was sort of floating around in my head but I've been kind of distracted because of these other … I've been thinking a lot about the *funeral* actually.

KELLY. Uh-huh?

PETER. Just how weird it was.

KELLY. Yeah.

PETER. No one really talking.

KELLY. Mm. No one knew what to *say.*

PETER. About?

KELLY. Just — you know, the shock. Everyone was in shock.

PETER. Okay. I thought you meant — knew what to say, like, weren't sure what to say because it seemed like maybe what happened wasn't what the military was saying.

KELLY. Oh.

PETER. Did you feel that at all? I don't know, maybe I'm crazy, but I felt that underneath a little, that people kind of thought it

10

wasn't an accident maybe, and that's why everyone was so quiet.

KELLY. Well. The way it was told to us — so many of his men saw it happen …

PETER. Yeah — I guess I thought maybe, because everyone there knew that Dad taught us, from the time we were little, how to shoot, how to handle weapons, that maybe some people didn't believe the story.

KELLY. Right. Well, the investigation was still going on at that point, it wasn't official, so some people might have felt that.

PETER. Yeah. And maybe it's a gun culture thing, we grew up around guns, you didn't, so it's something I would feel more than you … — *Target* practice, I just … Craig would always write about how careful he was with his weapon — I still can't picture it.

KELLY. It's a hard thing to picture. *(Pause.)*

PETER. Another thing that sucked was I could only be there for one *day*, remember? I had to fly back and do those stupid reshoots on my movie. The whole thing was so, it's like this *blur* — dealing with Mom, two years after Dad — and, like, the whole *gay* thing, do these people know, or not, and no one *talking* to me — except you.

KELLY. — How is your mom?

PETER. Oh, the same. I don't know what it will take to pierce that woman's heart, but … *(Pause.)*

KELLY. Well — I'm glad you're here. However. It's great to see you.

PETER. A bit weird maybe?

KELLY. Weird — a little. How you look.

PETER. Yeah, I always think of that … A relief, though, too.

KELLY. Uh-huh…?

PETER. That's how *I* feel. Even though it's hard. To finally see you again. — Not since the funeral, God! Even *spoken!*

KELLY. *Time.* I can't believe so much time has passed —

PETER. It feels like yesterday, right? — I wonder if the anniversary — because I wasn't aware of the exact date — if that had anything to do with what happened tonight.

KELLY. — What happened?

PETER. I … — I did something sort of shocking. *(Pause.)* I'm sorry.

KELLY. What?

PETER. I know I've already said this, but I can't believe I just showed up like this. Because — we talked, at the funeral, about what it was *like* for you when they just showed up and buzzed — and here I go do the exact same thing!

KELLY. — You didn't have my number, what other way could you have gotten in/touch?

PETER. I know, but still …

KELLY. It's fine. Really. Forget about it. *(Pause. Peter smiles.)*

PETER. Oh, all right, if you *insist* … *(Kelly smiles.)* Was it — is everything okay, I mean…?

KELLY. With…?

PETER. Did you have to change your numbers because of a client, did something happen?

KELLY. — Oh.

PETER. I always worried something *stalkery* would happen to you, you're so beautiful.

KELLY. — Oh!

PETER. I'm serious! Therapy, you know, two people alone in a room, it's very sexy! — Not that I've ever *done* it. In my fantasies — "the handsome doctor … "

KELLY. — You take sugar, right? I only have whole milk —

PETER. Plain is fine.

KELLY. Plain?

PETER. Yes — I'm playing this *assassin* in this movie I have coming up, I'm supposed to be getting in shape — I have this *trainer* …

KELLY. He's tough?

PETER. *She* — the guy trainers I've had, it's weird, I think they've all been jealous of me — my manager thinks it's because I'm so handsome. — But yes, she is tough.

KELLY. — It's funny, you know, you say what you imagine therapy is like — when I first started I thought I'd get to hear people talk about sex, their sex lives? But it's food. People want to talk about eating — their *body* image, their *eating* habits —

PETER. That's so pathetic.

KELLY. It's really what people are obsessed with.

PETER. Yeah, because nobody fucks anymore, they just eat like pigs instead! *(Pause.)*

KELLY. I don't know about that. Viagra's still pretty popular …

PETER. That's true I guess … — Right! There's your problem — the people who would have gone to therapy and talked about sex are all just popping Viagra instead!

KELLY. Huh …

PETER. — Oh, but, what about fucked-her-so-hard-she? *He* wanted to talk about sex. *(A moment. Then:)*

KELLY. — What?

PETER. It just came into my head, your client — we talked about him on Craig's last night. — That was what we called him, right? Fucked-her-so-/hard-she?

KELLY. — Wow, you remember that?

PETER. We talked about him half the night, how could I forget?! Coming up with our little theories about him — *Tim* thought he should go on Prozac, of course.

KELLY. — How *is* Tim? Nice to hear his name ...

PETER. Tim's well, he's well. Just went back to Los Angeles, yesterday actually — school's starting in a month, month and a half, so ...

KELLY. You guys were here...?

PETER. He just came to visit — I've been here — I'm doing a play...?

KELLY. — *That's* right.

PETER. *Long Day's Journey Into Night* —

KELLY. Of course — in the letter you — yes.

PETER. So ... he was out for the opening in April, then came back after school got out ... I've been here since *February*, God.

KELLY. — I remember now. So you've been here a while!

PETER. Yeah, it has been ...

KELLY. And Tim went back to get ready for school?

PETER. Another year of figuring out how to get inner-city eighth graders interested in *Romeo and Juliet*. Hopeless ...

KELLY. — You should go to his class, do a dramatic reading.

PETER. I suggested that! But he has this idea that it would be "disruptive." Since I'm "famous."

KELLY. I can see that.

PETER. Oh, please, my movie *tanked*. Did you see it?

KELLY. You know — I usually wait for the/DVD —

PETER. Oh God, it was *so* stinky — oh!

KELLY. Really? I've always been curious about that process — because I remember you said it was a good script. So how does it become a bad/movie?

PETER. Right — I was just about to start shooting, on Craig's last night, we talked about it ... — Why are we — who cares about my career, how boring!

KELLY. It's not boring to *me* —

PETER. To me it's like the least interesting — I guess we all get bored talking about work. Of course *I* want to know about fucked-her-so-hard-she, you probably find talking about *that* boring.

KELLY. — I can't believe you remember that. You have such/a good —

PETER. We had such an interesting debate on how you should handle him! *I* thought he was lying just to sound interesting, Tim thought he was self-medicating — Craig didn't think he was *lying,* just that he wanted to torture you — and didn't actually want to get better.

KELLY. Craig the expert —

PETER. Fucked-her-so-hard-she … What happened with him, how did things turn/out?

KELLY. — I have to say, I hated that nickname Craig gave him. It was so crass.

PETER. But — wasn't that how the guy himself — didn't he, say, like —

KELLY. It was how he would phrase his conquests —

PETER. Which is all he ever would talk about, right? And he would always use the same phrase — "I fucked her so hard she came six times."

KELLY. Yes —

PETER. "I fucked her so hard she started crying" — "I fucked her so hard she — woke up my ninety-year-old hearing-impaired neighbor" —

KELLY. Well — he didn't go *that* far. — You know, it slipped my mind a second ago — but I have to say — I read a number of just incredible reviews for the play. You opened in April you said? *(Peter makes "masturbation" motion.)* What.

PETER. — It's a terrible production.

KELLY. No. *(Peter nods.)* I had made a plan to come and just never got around/to it —

PETER. You're not missing anything.

KELLY. What's — wrong with it?

PETER. It's not true. *(Pause.)*

KELLY. I'm sorry to hear that.

PETER. Yeah. "Oh well!" *(Smiles.)* The "drama" is actually — I'm still kind of in shock I think — but the drama is that I walked off stage tonight — in the middle of the show. *(Pause.)*

KELLY. — Oh.

PETER. Yeah.

KELLY. I was going to — because I remember it being a pretty

long/play —
PETER. Yeah. *(Pause.)*
KELLY. — Is your tea okay…?
PETER. No, it's because there isn't any sugar. I don't want to drink it.
KELLY. Oh — would you like/some —
PETER. No — I can't. *(Pause.)* Yeah. Right before the intermission — my dad is calling me from offstage, "Come on, Edmund!" I make my exit and there he is — Tyrone, John Conrad — you know him, right? Very big/man —
KELLY. Mm-hmm —
PETER. So he sort of beckons me over, like, with this look on his face like he has a joke to tell me, or some little piece of gossip. So I go over, I lean into him, he grabs my shoulder and whispers into my ear, "I have a piece of advice for you." He says, "You're never —" *(Pause.)* He says, "You're never going to be a good actor till you stop sucking cock."
KELLY. — Oh.
PETER. Applause, act's over, I'm standing there *stunned,* he's looking at me and smiling this, this *smile,* and then he takes me, it's sort of like he's shoving me aside, but, like, *really* hard —
KELLY. Oh, Peter.
PETER. — I thought about going to the stage manager, telling her what happened, but John is the star, and no one else *saw* so he can just *lie* and — you know, in rehearsals, with John, and Scott, the director — I talked about *Dad* dying of leukemia, I talked about *Craig* dying in Iraq, I — and so I'm in my dressing room at this point, all alone, imagining having to go back out there with this man and pour my heart out to him and. — I looked in the mirror and I just grabbed my stuff and left. *(Pause.)*
KELLY. You did the right thing.
PETER. I didn't, though — I should have gone to the stage manager. I fucked up the whole second half of the/show.
KELLY. You can do all the formal stuff tomorrow — I'm sure you have an understudy.
PETER. *Drew.* He like does coke and gets escorts, I don't even think he knows the lines.
KELLY. Well. You'll straighten it out tomorrow. *(Pause.)*
PETER. Then the *other* thing is — I broke up with Tim last night.
KELLY. You broke up with/Tim? *(Peter's mobile rings, he checks it.)*

PETER. I should … *(Kelly nods. Peter gestures towards the bedroom. Kelly nods again. Peters answers the phone as he moves into the bedroom, off …)*

2.

Night. Kelly cleans up. Craig comes out of the bedroom, helps.

CRAIG. He's wasted.

KELLY. He's wasted? He didn't drink that much.

CRAIG. He's passed out …

KELLY. He just had two cups of coffee!

CRAIG. Yeah, with enough sugar to light up a room full of third graders.

KELLY. Well he *can't* be passed out for long.

CRAIG. It's ridiculous at his age. Ever since he was little — used to pour sugar on top of his Frosted Flakes, drove Dad crazy —

KELLY. *Ohhh.*

CRAIG. What.

KELLY. I bet he took a Xanax.

CRAIG. A Xanax?

KELLY. You were in the bathroom. Tim had Xanax for the plane, he hates flying.

CRAIG. What happened when I was in the bathroom?

KELLY. We were talking about Black Hawks —

CRAIG. Yeah —

KELLY. You got up to pee, and Tim said he couldn't imagine doing what you did because he couldn't even fly on a *commercial* plane without taking a Xanax. Then he took a bottle out of his pocket and shook it for effect.

CRAIG. "Shook it for effect"?

KELLY. It was cute.

CRAIG. So Peter took one?

KELLY. Not at the table — I'm just guessing — at some point.

CRAIG. But they're not prescribed to him. *(Pause.)*

KELLY. *Well …*

16

CRAIG. That's a powerful drug! He's not a doctor. I bet this shit flows in Hollywood/like fucking —
KELLY. One Xanax, I mean …
CRAIG. Yeah, one Xanax and he's so fucked up he can't even talk, he's in there *drooling. (Pause.)*
KELLY. So maybe he took two.
CRAIG. — Why are you being flip? You're against these drugs.
KELLY. In my *work* — when people medicate so they don't have to look at their problems — not as a once-in-a-while/thing.
CRAIG. I'm going to Fort Benning in the morning and now I can't even say goodbye to him! *(Pause.)*
KELLY. I'm sorry. How are you feeling?
CRAIG. A little agitated. I mean I'm *fine* … How are you?
KELLY. All things considered …
CRAIG. Yeah? *(Pause.)* I guess it was a nice night.
KELLY. It was.
CRAIG. He was nervous, but — I thought he'd be much worse.
KELLY. Peter or Tim?
CRAIG. Peter.
KELLY. You really do overestimate his attachment to you.
CRAIG. I know you think that —
KELLY. I think you need to be on the outside to see it. He's not seven anymore, copying the way you walk and talk. Look at when we were talking about Iraq — we really got into it!
CRAIG. *(A realization.)* I think *I* was more nervous than I expected.
KELLY. Really? You didn't seem nervous to me.
CRAIG. No?
KELLY. At most I would say — you were a little more "animated" than usual.
CRAIG. I thought it got most intense when we were talking about his career. That's where I felt maybe I went too far.
KELLY. — It's amazing, isn't it? Peter's gonna be a movie star! He's gonna be rich!
CRAIG. That movie sounded so fucking offensive.
KELLY. Yeah, but I agree with Peter, within the confines of what they/make today —
CRAIG. That's the thing. You start telling yourself/that —
KELLY. — But think why we don't have any Brandos or James Deans anymore — they're not, it's all so corporate-controlled, nobody's writing parts that a Brando or a — imagine Marlon

Brando doing *Titanic.* James Dean in *Lord of the Rings,* I mean —

CRAIG. But I'm talking about — yes, all the capitalist, corporate, I know Peter's not going to be in *Rebel Without a Cause* his first movie out — but I'm talking about Peter saying he thought the movie was *good. That's* what makes/me —

KELLY. Within the *confines* of what they produce today.

CRAIG. But that's exactly what — why can't he just say, "It's a bad movie, it's a piece of shit, but I have to start somewhere." What does that mean, "good within the confines"? You could say that about any movie, basically. Peter's too smart to start thinking that/way —

KELLY. Well, we don't know anything about the movie.

CRAIG. Yeah, but from what he said — "special forces" — "covert operations" — come on. I mean, do the movie, fine, but don't trick yourself about what it is. *(Pause.)*

KELLY. I think it was a good night.

CRAIG. Yeah … Yeah. Why not. Let's call it a good night.

KELLY. It was.

CRAIG. Just … I wanted to say goodbye in a more formal way.

KELLY. — So wake him up.

CRAIG. Nah, moment's gone. *(Pause.)*

KELLY. — You brought up fucked-her-so-hard-she, that threw me for a loop.

CRAIG. Oh God — it just came out …

KELLY. Out of *nowhere* …

CRAIG. I was thinking out loud. — I was pretty drunk there, till you put the coffee on.

KELLY. Why were you thinking about *him?*

CRAIG. Just — I don't know, you're seeing him in the morning …

KELLY. So?

CRAIG. Just — crossed my mind *(Pause.)*

KELLY. I forgot for a second.

CRAIG. What?

KELLY. Morning … *(Pause.)*

CRAIG. — At least it got Tim talking, finally.

KELLY. What?

CRAIG. Fucked-her-so-hard-she. Tim thought he was "clinically depressed."

KELLY. He was very articulate, I thought.

CRAIG. No, yeah — I liked him. Did you like him?

KELLY. Oh, definitely! They're great together.

CRAIG. Yeah … A little quiet …

KELLY. I'm sure he was *nervous* — meeting his boyfriend's identical *twin* —

CRAIG. No, I know … — You didn't think anything was off with him?

KELLY. No, not at all.

CRAIG. I don't know, I had this little nagging, like — just this feeling that something was off. Like — like I couldn't picture them fucking.

KELLY. — Craig!

CRAIG. Just, the vibe wasn't — whatever, he's better than The Psychopath.

KELLY. Oh, Craig.

CRAIG. I know you have a soft spot for him —

KELLY. I actually don't — but Adam was not a psychopath. He had *quirks,* he had *issues* —

CRAIG. Quirks?

KELLY. Whatever you want to call them. His personality was *affected* by the abuse he suffered. That doesn't make/him a —

CRAIG. — The abuse he *claimed* to have suffered.

KELLY. Well, we don't know if he did or not.

CRAIG. Wait — I thought you told Peter it never happened, the abuse. After Adam dumped him.

KELLY. I told Peter it was *possible* it never happened. I/can't —

CRAIG. That's not what he told me — he told me you told him you thought Adam made it up.

KELLY. Well … that's not what I said.

CRAIG. So you think it's possible that Adam's older brother forced him to give blow jobs to all the boys in the neighborhood, every day after school for two years, when he was six years/old —

KELLY. I think it's unlikely. But what I told Peter is that the memories could be an elaboration of something *less* severe that *did* happen. Or a fantasy that he got mixed up with reality because he was so young at the time/he —

CRAIG. — Or a lie. Meant to make Peter feel guilty, so he'd never dump Adam.

KELLY. Or that. — The point is, even if it isn't in any way *literally* true, the fact that Adam goes around telling people that this happened means he feels that something traumatic *did* happen to him when he was a boy, and that this "story" is the only way he has of communicating that trauma. You know, his parents were clearly very/disturbed —

CRAIG. See — this is what worries me about you. You're the same way with fucked-her-so-hard-she, you're so passive, or finding/ways to —

KELLY. — Can you stop calling him that now?

CRAIG. — What?

KELLY. It was one thing when it was just between us, but — he's a human being.

CRAIG. I'm just saying — if you know someone is manipulating you, then you should tell them, Look, I know what you're doing, stop it.

KELLY. Even if he *were* manipulating me — if I said that, he would never come back to therapy!

CRAIG. So what! At least this way he would know, he would have to walk around knowing that someone knew the truth!

KELLY. The purpose of therapy is to help someone change, not just/face the truth —

CRAIG. That's what I'm saying — people like that don't want to change, they just want to see what they can get away with —

KELLY. — Stop. *(Pause.)* This always happens when we talk seriously about my work.

CRAIG. We don't talk seriously about your work.

KELLY. Exactly,/because

CRAIG. Okay —

KELLY. you treat me like I'm this ridiculous person. Which does not make me feel *good,* or *loved,*/or —

CRAIG. Okay —

KELLY. Every time we talk about therapy or money, you get revved up, you/start getting —

CRAIG. Money?

KELLY. Yes — like tonight, when Tim started talking about his upbringing, you did the exact same thing you used to do when Adam would talk about growing up on the Upper East Side, or going to Horace/Mann —

CRAIG. Adam — /no —

KELLY. You turned off. You did. I think *that's* what was "off" to you about Tim — that he comes from money. It's why you have problems with my *dad,* it's why *therapy*/bothers you —

CRAIG. Problems with your dad?

KELLY. — When you criticize his lifestyle, his/attitude —
CRAIG. My problem with your dad is that he didn't love you. And the thing that was off to me about Tim — was that they didn't leave together. *(Pause.)*
KELLY. I did think that was weird. *(Pause.)* Maybe Peter wanted to say goodbye to you alone.
CRAIG. Then why did he — I don't know, something didn't feel right.
KELLY. I'm sure that's it. *(Pause.)*
CRAIG. — I also thought it was weird how much his phone kept ringing. Agents and managers call so late? How many times do they need to call? *(Pause.)*
KELLY. Speaking of late … *(Pause.)*
CRAIG. Yeah … *(Pause.)* — Okay. Do up the couch, I'll move Peter out/here —
KELLY. — What?
CRAIG. What?
KELLY. He's *staying?*
CRAIG. On the couch …
KELLY. Craig — I said, if he comes is this going to turn into an all-night thing? You said/no —
CRAIG. Kelly, he can't even —
KELLY. You said no. *Craig* —
CRAIG. Okay — *(Pause.)* Okay. I'll call him a car. *(Pause.)*
KELLY. Thank you. *(Pause. Craig kisses Kelly. He goes into the bedroom, off.)*

3.

Kelly watches TV. Peter comes out of the bedroom.

PETER. You painted!
KELLY. Oh — yeah.
PETER. White!
KELLY. Brighten things up …
PETER. It looks good. — I'm interrupting your *Law & Order.*

KELLY. Oh, I can watch it whenever.

PETER. Tivo?

KELLY. Yeah. I programmed it to record *Law & Order* whenever it's on — an endless/stream—

PETER. I see mine rerun all the time, it's so humiliating.

KELLY. You're kidding! Why have I never seen it?

PETER. Skater pothead: "Wha? Naw, man, I wasn't in the park that night."

KELLY. Very good!

PETER. *(Sitting.)* Please — the casting director just wanted to fuck me. I told him I couldn't skate, he said, Oh, it's okay, there's not much skating — they send me the shooting script, of course I'm on a skateboard in *every* scene.

KELLY. I used to not like *Law & Order*, but then it really started to grow on me.

PETER. Oh yeah?

KELLY. I have this theory about/it —

PETER. — When did you start watching all this TV, I don't remember you being a big TV person.

KELLY. Yeah, I never was before.

PETER. Was it after Craig died? *(Pause.)*

KELLY. Maybe — when I couldn't sleep I'd watch TV, I'd/watch

PETER. I had trouble sleeping —

KELLY. these shows —

PETER. The worst time for me was actually *months* after — when the official report came out that said it was an accident. After that I just couldn't sleep for some reason.

KELLY. Yeah, the grief comes at different times, it's so unpredictable. — But I came up with this theory — would you like to hear/it?

PETER. — Oh, definitely!

KELLY. Well, I realized that all these shows, all the *Law & Order*s and all the rip-offs, have the same exact structure: Someone dies, and a whole team of specialists springs up to figure out how to solve the mystery of the person's death.

PETER. Right?

KELLY. Which I think is a fantasy people have — that they won't be forgotten. That their death won't just be accepted and mourned, but that an entire *community* will come together, all these special people — lawyers and scientists and forensics experts, judges, detectives — who are devoted, who will not stop until the mystery

22

of the death is solved. And therefore symbolically reversed.

PETER. — Wow!

KELLY. Only took me six thousand episodes to figure it out.

PETER. Good use of *insomnia* ... — It's weird with me, lately — I've been *sleeping* fine, but then out of nowhere, doing the play, like — like the other night. I had this fantasy, this image almost, of a Black Hawk helicopter crashing through the ceiling of the theatre.

KELLY. — While you were onstage?

PETER. At the curtain call — and curtain calls have always been kind of weird for me, I sort of forget who I am — am I me, or am I the character? But lately, it's like — I feel like *Craig* in the curtain call. And I thought — well, it makes sense, that's how I started acting, when I was little, I would pretend that I was him ... So maybe it's a delayed grief reaction, like?

KELLY. — It may be ...

PETER. Tim thinks I have Post-Traumatic Stress Disorder, keeps bugging me to see his shrink. But I'm like, No — if this is grief, these "moments" — then I should feel it, right? I don't want to medicate my grief away ...

KELLY. I'm not a psychiatrist. But I think Tim is right, it does sound like you should see one.

PETER. Really, you think? Huh. That surprises me. I'll think about it then ... *(Pause.)* — I'm sorry — I feel a little silly asking this, but — are you moving? *(Pause.)*

KELLY. You mean — all the boxes—

PETER. Not that you wouldn't *tell* me, I/just —

KELLY. I felt like my life had a lot of clutter, that's all.

PETER. Oh, you're putting some things —

KELLY. In storage, clearing space ...

PETER. ... painting ...

KELLY. So ...

PETER. That's good ... — Hey, you know, I know I mentioned to you — I don't know if you remember — at the funeral? I mentioned Craig's emails? From Iraq?

KELLY. Yeah — I remember your mentioning them ...

PETER. I just realized, I actually have them with me. *(Pause.)*

KELLY. Uh-huh?

PETER. I keep them at the theatre, I read them before shows, and I just grabbed them before I left tonight. Sort of instinctively ...

KELLY. Right ...

PETER. I know — I remember at the funeral your telling me you and Craig didn't email while he was over there, you just talked on the phone — something about the distance …

KELLY. Email felt weird to me — not intimate.

PETER. Hearing his voice …

KELLY. Felt more —

PETER. Right, yeah. But it must — do you ever — now that he's gone, do you ever wish you had anything down on paper, that you could look at, or…?

KELLY. I have other things …

PETER. Yeah … I guess, too, you were used to distance. I mean — in a way it must seem like he might even be coming back. It's only been a year. He was active duty four years after you guys finished Harvard, that's such a long time to be away from each other —

KELLY. — Well, but I always knew that that would be over someday. There was a very definite timetable when he would be done. Plus he wasn't fighting. So it was always in the background that he'd be coming back … which — isn't the case anymore.

PETER. Right — and you were in grad school, and becoming a therapist, so you were also really busy then, you weren't as settled as you are now …

KELLY. Exactly.

PETER. I remember when he got called up again, I thought — because he had done his four years, it's like — I knew you go on Inactive Ready Reserves after, but I just assumed he was done. Starting his life finally, writing his dissertation … — He never complained, though — wouldn't apply for a deferment …

KELLY. He felt a lot of loyalty to the Army — ROTC paid for school. He couldn't have gone to Harvard without it.

PETER. Well, he also believed in the war. There was that also. *(Pause.)* I think it's so sad he never finished his Ph.D. Do you still have all his Faulkner research?

KELLY. I sent it to your mom.

PETER. Really? She never told me that. Typical. God, for a woman who wanted both her sons to get out of the Midwest, she's never stopped resenting us for it. She hasn't come to see my/*play* —

KELLY. — You think it's that?

PETER. What?

KELLY. You think she resents you because you left your —

PETER. Oh, the social class thing, definitely, anything to do with

24

being *educated, cultured* makes her — I think that was a big reason she didn't — not that she didn't, doesn't *like* you,/but —

KELLY. But isn't it also — very generally, that she resents that her life didn't turn out the way she planned, her husband dying, her son — I mean, she pushed you and Craig very hard in school, didn't she? So you could/get out of —

PETER. Oh, and took us to theatre, and took us to museums — but she didn't want us to be cultured so much as she just wanted us to be able to get away from Dad. When he got back from Vietnam I think she knew something was — even from pictures you can tell. But she wasn't going to leave him, they had us — so she pushed us to excel, go away to school ... but once we *did* that — she resented/us.

KELLY. I see. I thought maybe she hadn't told you about the dissertation because it reminds her of everything — that hasn't turned out right. *(Pause.)*

PETER. He was such a good writer. These emails — they could be published. I've thought about maybe trying to make them into a one-man show. I don't know if I'd play him. I guess it would make the most sense for me to, but — feels a little — also — they're so intimate, I don't know if I'd want to share them with people. I haven't shown them to anyone. *(Pause.)* I'd — love to share them with you if you ...

KELLY. Oh. That's ... you know, I just don't think I'm ready. *(Pause.)*

PETER. I understand. *(Pause.)* You can really see in them how much he learned from you, I think ... just, his emotions and ... it's hard because, you didn't know him before you met him obviously, but — the way he blossomed with you — especially after you got married ... God, it's just about three years, right?

KELLY. Just about. September ...

PETER. Wow. I remember when you guys finally got engaged, him calling me up to tell me — God, I was so happy. Because I was getting, I was definitely, like, Let's hurry it up here!

KELLY. We had always talked about it — he just wanted to wait till he was done with active duty.

PETER. — I also think Dad getting sick definitely — gave him some perspective ... And 9/11 ... *(Pause.)*

KELLY. — Was that your director who called before? Is/everything —

PETER. — No, I haven't called him back yet, he just left me a voice mail — I was talking to Tim, actually. He's emailing me all this information on PTSD, so ... *(Pause.)*

KELLY. I owe you an apology, Peter.

PETER. — Uh-huh?

KELLY. I know how important it was to you that I stay in touch. I told you at the funeral that I would — and I didn't.

PETER. Oh, thank you ... no, definitely, I mean — I'd be lying if I said ... — part of me, you know, definitely did the play hoping being in the same city would make us ... you know, even if it meant going away from Tim, and pissing off my agents ... make us close again. *(Pause.)*

KELLY. Your letter really — it really did touch me. I should have responded.

PETER. ... I knew it was a really big thing I was proposing, so I kind of — I expected you to say "No," or at least — that you'd need time to think about it ... — But — yeah, you know? I asked you to have a *baby*, I mean, *some* kind of acknowledgement —

KELLY. I know. *(Pause.)*

PETER. — I hate to do this, but I should call Scott back before it gets too late, is that okay?

KELLY. — Sure.

PETER. Thanks. *(Peter takes out his mobile and goes back into the bedroom.)*

4.

Craig comes out of the bedroom.

KELLY. Hey.

CRAIG. So, I don't think Peter's gonna make it home tonight. *(Pause.)*

KELLY. Why not.

CRAIG. I've been trying to get him up for fifteen/minutes —

KELLY. Craig —

CRAIG. I don't know what else to/do.

KELLY. Wake him up. *(Pause.)* Call a car, I'll help you get/him —

CRAIG. — What's the big deal if he just crashes on the couch?

KELLY. *I don't want him here. (Pause.)*

CRAIG. You don't want him/here.

KELLY. I don't want him/here.

CRAIG. Why don't you/want him —

KELLY. — All right, what's happening. *(Pause.)*

CRAIG. What.

KELLY. Something is happening —

CRAIG. So say it then, what.

KELLY. You don't want to be alone with me. *(Pause.)*

CRAIG. That's not true, Kelly. I'm going to *Iraq,* my brother/is —

KELLY. You're going to *Georgia.*

CRAIG. — I'm going to Georgia, and then I'm going to Iraq. What, you think I'm being dramatic?

KELLY. Yes, I do.

CRAIG. — Look, he's not — I don't feel right just throwing him in a car —

KELLY. Why not.

CRAIG. Because I think — he's scared, and I don't think he should have to wake up alone in the morning/like I —

KELLY. — You keep saying he's scared — we talked about the war half the night, he didn't sound scared at all. He sounded very confident —

CRAIG. We were talking about politics, not me leaving.

KELLY. — But if he was so scared, I really don't think he would have been able to disagree with you the way he/did.

CRAIG. That's not even — he was just putting on a show for Tim. *(Pause.)*

KELLY. — What?

CRAIG. Tim's against the war, so — whatever, the point is, whatever he said/when we were —

KELLY. No, what do you mean, "putting on a show"?

CRAIG. Tim's — that's actually not how Peter feels, Peter is not "against" the war, he was just saying that for Tim's sake.

KELLY. What...?

CRAIG. He — Peter told me that because *Tim* marches against the war, and because all their *friends* are against it, it's just easier for him to keep quiet about how he really feels.

KELLY. So — everything he was saying — was/just —

CRAIG. — His feelings are complicated. He's against the administration, but the actual war he thinks is worth fighting. Tim doesn't feel that way, *obviously,*/so —

KELLY. Wait — is *that* what this is about?

CRAIG. What.

KELLY. Are you acting this way because I agreed with Tim? *(Pause.)*

CRAIG. Acting what way.

KELLY. Not wanting to be alone with me —

CRAIG. Kelly, I *do* want to be alone with/you —

KELLY. I could tell you were getting pissed, I just thought it was something to do with Tim. — Is that why you were so pissed off? Because I was/saying that —

CRAIG. — We *have* never really talked about the war in the terms we did tonight.

KELLY. — Yes we have.

CRAIG. — *I* recall your saying to me that it would be good for Saddam to be out of power — when the war started. You disagreed with how we got into it, but you felt the Iraqis/would benefit —

KELLY. — What?

CRAIG. When we watched Tony Blair with Bush, remember? You said how articulate he was —

KELLY. Craig, I said it was a *fake* war that they were *lying* about to get us into —

CRAIG. You don't remember when we watched Blair?

KELLY. I was — *theoretically,* we were talking about human rights in *general* —

CRAIG. And I remember you more or less agreeing with me.

KELLY. I was sympathetic — in the *abstract* — to the "idea" of human rights, I mean, what, did you expect me to argue for Saddam Hussein? Oh, this is ridiculous, you're purposefully/misremembering! *(A mobile phone rings once. Both look vaguely to it. Pause.)* — Now I'm wondering what *else* I've said to you that you're unclear on.

CRAIG. What does *that* mean.

KELLY. I'm wondering about our having a *baby* … *(Pause.)*

CRAIG. What about it.

KELLY. I don't know! I thought we were/clear about —

CRAIG. We just talked about it tonight — when I get back, when I finish/school —

KELLY. In front of *Peter.*

CRAIG. What …

KELLY. — *Peter* brought it up, *Peter* asked if we were going to have a baby — were you saying it just to please him?

CRAIG. Kelly, we've talked about this a hundred times — I want to wait till I'm teaching, I don't want to take any more money from your father.

KELLY. I still don't see what the big deal is —

CRAIG. The big deal is, he's a *cock. (Pause.)* — Jesus! We talked about starting a family — sitting right on this couch, looking out at the *cloud of death* hanging over/the city —

KELLY. — Please, please don't invoke/that —

CRAIG. Why not? That day is seared into my — every single thing we said to one/another!

KELLY. — You know what? I'm tired, I want to go to sleep. I'll sleep on the couch — *(Goes to couch.)* go sleep with your brother.

CRAIG. — Oh, fuck you! *(Craig gets his keys, moves to apartment door.)*

KELLY. Where are you going?

CRAIG. For a walk.

KELLY. Craig — *(Craig opens door.)* Craig — don't go — *(Craig stops. Pause. Kelly approaches him. He shuts door. Turns. Pause. Kelly leans in, kisses Craig. Pause. He kisses back. The kiss grows ... Mobile phone rings once. Craig looks to it. Kelly keeps kissing him. Craig detaches himself and goes to the phone. Picks it up. Pause.)* — What?

CRAIG. *(Reads:)* "Did Tim leave yet. Horny." *(Craig looks up at Kelly.)* Adam. *(Pause.)*

KELLY. — You don't know what it means. It could just be a — like a joke or something.

CRAIG. A *joke?*

KELLY. Like he teases him by sending him texts like that. *(Pause.)* What. *(Pause.)* What. *(Craig looks at the phone again a moment, then puts it down. He gets up, goes to kitchen, opens cabinet, drawer ...)* What are you — *(Craig grabs a pot and a spoon, goes into the bedroom, off. Kelly stands. Offstage sounds of the spoon hitting the pot loudly. After some time Peter comes out of the bedroom. Stumbles. Sees Kelly, smiles.)*

PETER. Hey ... sorry ... *(Peter grabs jacket, starts to go. Kelly sees phone.)*

KELLY. — Don't forget your phone — I think someone might have texted you while you were asleep.

PETER. — Oh. *(Pause. Kelly goes into the bedroom, off. Peter takes phone from pocket, checks it. Then goes out the door, off. Pause. The*

29

bedroom door opens. Craig comes out, goes to the couch, curls into it. Grips himself tight. Pause. Kelly follows.)

KELLY. Craig. *(Pause.)* Craig, what's happening. *(Moves to Craig. He curls more tightly into himself, burrows deeper into the couch. Kelly turns and goes back into the bedroom, off.)*

5.

Kelly watches TV. Peter comes out of the bedroom.

PETER. Jon Stewart!

KELLY. *(Turns.)* My other Tivo favorite.

PETER. Yeah, he's funny. But it's weird — I was at a party a couple nights ago? And this guy starts saying Bush is as bad as Hitler. *Then* he starts talking about how hilarious *The Daily Show* is. And I thought — if you were in Germany in the 1930s, would you watch a show where some smartass made fun of Hitler? Little mustache jokes while he's throwing Jews in the ovens? I mean if you really think George Bush is evil, then how can you laugh at "George Bush is dumb" jokes?

KELLY. It's the sensibility. The sensibility comes closer to conveying the truth than the real news does, I think that's what people respond to.

PETER. Yeah, but whose truth is being conveyed? Jon Stewart has so much privilege, I think it's a pretty small slice of the "truth" he's conveying. Like when I watch him make fun of evangelicals — if you really care about the truth, you can't just speak to your own tiny group, you have to figure out how to speak to the community.

KELLY. The community…?

PETER. People who may not be like you but that you still have — something in common with. A basic humanity. Even if they *do* believe in God, or believe in the war in Iraq. Go to the Indiana State Fair — those are the people we need to figure out how to talk to. They're not going away, we can't just make fun of them. Don't you think?

KELLY. But aren't they beyond reach? These people think the

Rapture is coming. They think people like us are going to burn in hell — literally.

PETER. But that's the — that was one thing about Craig. He could talk to those Army guys like — it didn't matter, Harvard, all the books he read — he never forgot where he came from. He knew that these people, whatever insane things they believed — he thought you could reach into the core of them, and find something deeper and truer than all the surface stuff, God and politics and all that.

KELLY. I don't know — God and politics go pretty deep.

PETER. *(Mostly conceding.)* Yes and no ...

KELLY. He thought we could reach the Iraqis too. Do you think he was right about that? *(Pause.)*

PETER. I hear you. I just don't want to write people off, I guess. — I mean, how do you feel as a therapist? Someone comes to you with all these problems, doing all these bad things to themselves, to other people ... you have to believe that there's a way to reach them, right? No matter how awful or crazy they seem ... *(Pause.)*

KELLY. No, I agree ... — What did your director say, is everything okay?

PETER. — I chickened out, I still haven't called him. I was just leaving messages for my agents, and my manager, and my lawyer.

KELLY. — Your publicist is out of town?

PETER. I really should have gone to the stage manager.

KELLY. I think you're the last person who needs to be questioning his actions tonight —

PETER. I've kind of been — I don't know ... Scott — the director — on opening night ... — Tim had left the party, he doesn't like staying out late — and I was really drunk, and Tim doesn't have much of a sex drive because of the Paxil and — I ended up following Scott into the bathroom — and — Drew, my understudy — came into the bathroom and saw — Scott blowing me basically. So ... — I'm sure word got around to the company, I'm sure John heard ...

KELLY. — Oh. *(Pause.)*

PETER. And — I might as well just put it all out there — I've been sleeping with Adam still. — So basically, that's my life. *(Pause.)* You're moving, aren't you. *(Pause. Kelly turns off the TV. She looks at Peter, nods.)* When.

KELLY. Next week.

PETER. Next *week.* Where?

31

KELLY. I have a good friend from school, in Ann Arbor. She's just been through a divorce. I'm going to go up there for a while.

PETER. What about your practice?

KELLY. I referred everyone. *(Pause.)*

PETER. Why couldn't you ... did I *do* something that made you not want to talk to me,/or —

KELLY. It's just me. I haven't wanted contact with anybody. *(Pause.)* I didn't know you were in this much pain, Peter. I'm sorry.

PETER. Oh, it's all — drama, I'm fine, really. I'm so sorry *you've* been — I mean I figured things were tough, that's why you hadn't ... — I think I had the idea because, just, being in the play made me — I had all these hopes going into it, but it turned out to be like *Long Day's Journey to the Hamptons* — actors constantly checking messages, luxurious spreads of pastries at every rehearsal, Scott taking up all this time telling stories about which Hollywood actors have big dicks — I wanted to scream! The play is like being in a *war,* these people are trying to kill each other — literally! My father won't spend money on treatment for my TB, for the sanitarium! And no one was taking it seriously ... So I sort of — would retreat into my own little world, and read Craig's emails ... they were so inspiring, I mean, just — this extraordinary thing of him turning against the war, you know? And I kept thinking of the two of you, how much you had wanted a/child —

KELLY. — Turning against the war?

PETER. Yeah — Did you — I was wondering if that was something he could even talk about —

KELLY. Not — there were limits to what he could say, he/wasn't —

PETER. So you had no — Oh, Kelly — reading the emails is like — this *awakening,* it's like the birth of this whole other person! I know you said you're not ready — but if you ever do want to read them — just — please — anytime ...

KELLY. Thank you — I might someday. *(Pause. Peter smiles at Kelly. Looks away.)*

PETER. — It's late, I should get going. Big day tomorrow, God only/knows —

KELLY. Are you — where are/you — *(Peter goes to his bag.)*

PETER. — If you have email in Ann Arbor, I really would like to stay in/touch —

KELLY. — It's late, stay here. *(Kelly looks at Peter. Pause.)*

PETER. — Okay!

KELLY. — Take the bedroom. In the morning I'll make some pancakes.

PETER. Eeek, pancakes.

KELLY. — Oh, right. What can you — I can make them without/sugar —

PETER. Ah, fuck it — pancakes! With *gobs* of maple syrup — *(They laugh. Pause.)* I'm — glad we could be honest with each other.

KELLY. Me too.

PETER. Yeah. — Just — gonna use the bathroom … *(Peter goes into the bathroom, off. Kelly takes the bed sheet off the box and goes to the couch. Sees Peter's bag. Goes to it, unzips it, looks in. Begins to reach in. Toilet flushes. Kelly zips up the bag, moves away. Peter comes out of the bathroom, takes his bag.)* You know — I really don't mind sleeping on the couch …

KELLY. Please — take the bedroom.

PETER. You sure?

KELLY. I'm sure.

PETER. Okay. — G'night. *(Peter moves towards the bedroom.)*

KELLY. Can I … — *(Peter turns.)* I think part of my hesitation with — the emails, your asking if you could share them with me before — I think because they were written to *you* I feel — that it's really not/my —

PETER. — Oh, no, I'm *sure* Craig would have wanted me to share them with you. *(Pause.)*

KELLY. Then I think I — I would like to/read them if it's —

PETER. Oh, of course, absolutely. *(Opens bag.)* There's one in particular I've most wanted you to … *(Picks one.)* I *think* this is the — they all blur together a little … *(Sits down, as if to begin reading. Kelly does not move to sit.)*

KELLY. — Oh.

PETER. Is it okay if I read it to you?

KELLY. It's not — I can read it.

PETER. Oh, you'd rather … I just thought it would be — I guess I'm so eager to *share* … *(Pause.)*

KELLY. If you'd — sure.

PETER. Is that okay?

KELLY. — Sure. *(Kelly sits.)*

PETER. Okay. If it gets to be too much or anything — just tell me, I'll stop. *(Pause. Reads:)* "Abu Ghraib is already a punch line; I'll spare you the jokes. For about five minutes we all felt the truth of it but that feeling got swept away in the hot desert wind like every other emotion here." — A little Faulknerian. "From what I can tell, it's not a big deal at home either. I think the images are a real comfort to people — that we're the powerful ones, in control, alive, clothed. I had a memory the other night of the time Dad put his fist through the car windshield. Do you remember? I recall so vividly Mom telling us when she was taking us to school the next day that it was a Vietnam flashback. We couldn't have been older than six. We were coming back from dinner, Dad was driving, Mom was saying something to him — and suddenly there was a crunch. I looked up and the windshield was like a spider web, and there was Dad's bleeding fist, gripping the steering wheel tight … I looked over at Mom and I remember thinking that she was going to look a certain way, upset or scared … but instead I saw her grinning. A little creeping grin on her face. You were looking out the window like you hadn't noticed anything, so I punched you in the arm. You said, "Ow," and Dad looked back for a second, then turned back to the road. I think I've remembered this now, after so many years, because what I learned in that instant — that to be married to a man so powerful he could put his fist through glass was what made our mother smile — is exactly how I feel here: so powerful I can't stop smiling, while suffering a wound I do not feel." *(Pause. Peter looks up.)*

KELLY. — Jesus.

PETER. No memory.

KELLY. — You don't remember that at all?

PETER. Vague memory of Craig hitting me and Dad not doing anything. But that happened all the time.

KELLY. — Craig would hit you?

PETER. It was weird. When Dad would hit me, Craig would yell at him to stop. But then Craig would hit me a lot too. When I would go tell Dad, he wouldn't do anything. And when I would go tell Mom, she would say, "Go tell your father." *(Pause.)*

KELLY. I'm sorry.

PETER. Oh, you know, everyone has a childhood. — Craig told me once — your dad abused you?

KELLY. Emotionally.

PETER. He was never really specific …

KELLY. Neither was my father.

PETER. You mean …

KELLY. He wasn't around, he was having affairs, he bought me lots of things I didn't want … my mother was on too much Valium to care.

PETER. I'm sorry. *(Kelly nods. Pause.)* Is this okay? Should I/keep —

KELLY. Please.

PETER. It's very eloquent, isn't it?

KELLY. It's beautiful.

PETER. A bit purple here and there … *(Peter looks back at the paper, reads.)* "The malaise among the men has taken a turn. It's clear to everyone now that we are not equipped to bring this country back to life. The city is dying, and we are the ones killing it. But I do not blame my men. They were told they would be heroes bringing freedom, and instead have been told to invade people's homes and take their freedom. They are ordered to protect themselves from violence by actively doing violence, which leads to more violence to protect themselves against: No sane person could survive these tasks. I have begun to wonder if I myself will recover from who I have become here in just a few short months. But then in quieter moments I find myself thrown back into memories of who I was before and am faced with the realization that the horror I feel here is not … — " Hmmm. *(Pause.)* This sort of goes on for a while, there was a part at the end —

KELLY. No, please, keep reading.

PETER. — Reading out loud it's longer than I … there's a, where is the/part —

KELLY. — Go back, what was he saying about the "horror" — "the realization that the horror I feel here" — I want to hear that. *(Pause. Peter looks at the paper.)*

PETER. "But then in quieter moments I find myself thrown back into memories of who I was before and am faced with the realization that the horror I feel here is not … something I fully understand … It is unclear which way the narrative of this war will twist next. Faulkner understood that the psychological legacy of war is that/the individual" —

KELLY. — Are you skipping something?

PETER. No. No.

KELLY. The — read it again? *(Pause.)*

PETER. I think — that part might have been something he meant just for me, actually. *(Pause.)*

KELLY. What are you skipping?

PETER. It's not really — *(Kelly takes the email from Peter and reads it. She looks up. Pause.)* I think he — I think he meant just fantasies, or —

KELLY. *Fantasies?*

PETER. He says "need," need's not — I mean Fort Benning was probably anxiety, but —

KELLY. *(Reads.)* " — in quieter moments I find myself thrown back into memories of who I was before and am faced with the realization that the horror I feel here is not just a consequence of the war, but is horror of the core of me, of who I have always been. In fact I have felt more clear-headed here than ever before. I haven't felt the overwhelming need to sexually demean women that has haunted me my entire life, and haven't fucked since leaving Fort Benning." *(Puts down email.)* Every *night* I let him fuck me — every night of my/ *life!*

PETER. — I don't — I don't think/he's saying —

KELLY. — Did you know he fucked other women. *(Long pause.)*

PETER. One time —

KELLY. — I knew it —

PETER. we were — do you want me/to —

KELLY. Yes.

PETER. — We were in a bar, we were drunk, he went to the bathroom — he was gone awhile, so when he came back I just said, "Are you okay." Like maybe he was throwing up … *(Pause.)* He said, "I think the bitch bit me." *(Pause.)*

KELLY. "I think the bitch bit me."

PETER. I just thought he/was joking —

KELLY. — I knew when he wouldn't apply for a deferment. I knew —

PETER. — I think it's like, it's the violence just finally got to him, you know?/ The —

KELLY. It has nothing to do with, no — he said, it's who he's *always* been —

PETER. No, that's what I mean — like — five years old, Dad took us shooting, there's photo albums of dead animals/all —

KELLY. Don't blame this on your father, it's/not —

PETER. He loved you so much, Kelly —

KELLY. — He was a coward!

PETER. — He fucking shot his head off, right? He obviously felt guilty!

KELLY. Guilt? Over *me?* No, that's not guilt,/no —

36

PETER. What is it then?

KELLY. — He wanted to get *away* from me!

PETER. — What?

KELLY. He wanted to get away from/me,

PETER. No —

KELLY. so he went to Iraq and *shot himself* — oh! *(Kelly rises.)* Leave my house I need to be alone —

PETER. — Kelly — *(Kelly goes into bedroom, off. Peter stays seated.)*

6.

Craig is on the couch. Near dawn. Kelly opens the bedroom door, comes out a few steps.

CRAIG. Hey.

KELLY. You're talking. *(Pause.)*

CRAIG. I have to leave/in a —

KELLY. I know what time it is. *(Pause. Kelly comes to the couch, sits.)*

CRAIG. Get any sleep? *(Kelly shakes her head "no." Craig smiles.)* Thinking about fucked-her-so-hard-she? *(Pause.)*

KELLY. Why would I be thinking about him.

CRAIG. You're seeing him. *(Pause.)*

KELLY. No. I am not thinking/about —

CRAIG. Call the bluff.

KELLY. — What?

CRAIG. Tell him you know what he's doing. Every time you listen to him go on about one of these women he's getting/off on it —

KELLY. You have never met him. Yes, he is exasperating. But he is a human being, with a history, who is in pain — who is communicating his/pain

CRAIG. He's *acting* like he's in pain —

KELLY. in the only way he knows. He's trying to make me feel small, so I can know how *he* feels: small.

CRAIG. No, he's just trying to make you feel small. And he'll keep doing it until you crack, and then he'll leave.

KELLY. — We have very different views of human nature. *(Pause.)*

Do you love me, Craig? *(Pause.)*
CRAIG. I don't think we should have a serious discussion right now.
KELLY. Why not.
CRAIG. I'm not capable of it. I'm stressed —
KELLY. Things have come up tonight. We can't/just —
CRAIG. I think saying anything is a bad idea.
KELLY. — I think you should be able to answer the question. *(Pause.)* Do you love me. *(Pause.)* Did you?
CRAIG. Did I what.
KELLY. Did you ever love me. *(Pause.)*
CRAIG. Of course.
KELLY. Of course?
CRAIG. Of course I loved you.
KELLY. Loved? *(Pause.)* When did you stop. *(Pause.)* When did/you —
CRAIG. After we got married. I knew it was a mistake. I knew I didn't love you. *(Pause. Kelly cries. She punches Craig repeatedly. She stops. Pause.)* I have to get dressed. *(Pause. Craig goes into the bedroom, off. Kelly hyperventilates. Calms some. Picks up her phone, goes to her phone book, dials.)*
KELLY. Hi, this is a message for Bradley. It's Kelly Conners calling. I'm sorry to be calling so early and with such short notice. I need to cancel this morning's session. I'm very sorry. I'll see you at our regular time next week. Take care.

7.

Peter is on the couch asleep, a script open before him. Bedroom door opens, Kelly comes out. Pause. She looks at Peter. Goes into the kitchen and runs water, opens cabinets, makes noise. Peter wakes up. Sees Kelly. She sees him.

PETER. Sorry … *(Kelly makes tea. Peter looks at the box of books.)* I was looking over one of my speeches — "It was a great mistake, my being born a man" — I got inspired by all of Craig's books. I must have passed out … Melville, Hawthorne, Hemingway,

Faulkner ... I remember in high school Craig was reading *A Farewell to Arms*. He said it was a war novel — I thought it was about a double amputee ... God, America had so many great writers ... *(Kelly continues making tea.)* — Oh, shit, what time is it?

KELLY. — Nine.

PETER. Phew — I have a company meeting at ten. Spoke to Scott — told him what happened, he talked to John, John I guess feels terrible ... Sounds like we'll all kiss and make up. *(Pause. Peter looks at Kelly.)* I'm sure this won't make — much of a difference to you, but — I'm really sorry about what happened last night.

KELLY. — Thank you, I accept your apology. *(Kelly straightens things up in the kitchen. Peter looks at the couch.)*

PETER. — I'm gonna miss this couch! I remember, on 9/11 — I had just moved to L.A., and I remember calling here, all day, I couldn't get through till late in the night — Craig picked up the phone, and I remember this peace in his voice — telling me about how you two just sat on the couch all day — looking out the window, at the cloud, holding each other ... When I think of 9/11, that's always the picture I have ... *(Kelly does not respond.)* — *That's* what I forgot to ask you! Whatever happened to fucked-her-so-hard-she?

KELLY. — He stopped coming.

PETER. Why?

KELLY. I had to cancel a session, and he never came again.

PETER. Huh. I had this whole fantasy that he was why you changed your numbers, like he was stalking you/or something — *(Kelly stops.)*

KELLY. I changed my numbers because of you. *(Pause.)*

PETER. Because of *me?*

KELLY. Peter, you've invaded my home, no warning, you come in here, you/read me

PETER. I didn't have your numbers —

KELLY. this email — say what you will, you did it. So please — just say goodbye, and leave. *(Pause.)*

PETER. When did you change them, after getting my letter?

KELLY. I just want to start over.

PETER. I don't understand, what did I do?

KELLY. I just told you: I wanted to start over.

PETER. But — there was no one I could talk to about him, you were/the —

KELLY. There are therapists.

PETER. But — I love you. *(Pause.)*

KELLY. Bye. *(Pause.)*

PETER. *Fine. (He grabs his bag, starts to go, then stops.)* — For you. *(He puts the emails down on the couch.)*

KELLY. — How *dare* you — no! *(Peter goes, off. Pause. Kelly turns to the window. The sun is shining, sounds of the city coming to life. She looks out the window. Craig comes out of the bedroom, in uniform, with luggage.)*

CRAIG. It's time for me to go. *(Kelly turns. Pause. Craig goes to the couch and sits. He cries. Kelly goes to the couch and sits. After a time:)*

KELLY. Listen. I think you were right. I think this stress is — it was a mistake to talk. I don't think this is who we really/are —

CRAIG. I have to go, I/can't —

KELLY. I know you do. We'll talk when — phone, email, whatever you're most comfortable with, whenever you — we'll find a way to understand what's/happening —

CRAIG. I don't — I don't think that's a good idea. *(Pause.)*

KELLY. What's not.

CRAIG. Being in touch.

KELLY. Being in touch … at all? *(Pause.)*

CRAIG. I have to go.

KELLY. Craig — *(Craig rises. He gathers his things and goes to the door.)*

CRAIG. Goodbye. *(Pause. Craig goes, off. After a time, Kelly gets up and pours herself a cup of tea. She returns to the couch, turns on the TV. Puts on* The Daily Show. *A moment passes. She looks at the emails sitting on the couch. Pause. She picks up one, begins to read. She stops, puts it down. Pause. She goes to the box of books, opens it. Goes to the emails, picks them up. Places them in the box. Sits, begins placing books neatly into the box. On the television, sounds of Jon Stewart, laughter, applause …)*

End of Play

PROPERTIES LIST

Cardboard box with books
Bed sheet, pillow
Tea kettle, teabags, cups
Cell phones
Keys
Pot and spoon
Man's bag with e-mails
Phone book
Script
Luggage

SOUND EFFECTS

Front door buzzer
Law and Order on TV
Cell phone ring
The Daily Show on TV
Toilet flush
Running water
City sounds in morning
Jon Stewart, laughter, applause

NEW PLAYS

★ **GUARDIANS by Peter Morris.** In this unflinching look at war, a disgraced American soldier discloses the truth about Abu Ghraib prison, and a clever English journalist reveals how he faked a similar story for the London tabloids. "Compelling, sympathetic and powerful." *–NY Times.* "Sends you into a state of moral turbulence." *–Sunday Times (UK).* "Nothing short of remarkable." *–Village Voice.* [1M, 1W] ISBN: 978-0-8222-2177-7

★ **BLUE DOOR by Tanya Barfield.** Three generations of men (all played by one actor), from slavery through Black Power, challenge Lewis, a tenured professor of mathematics, to embark on a journey combining past and present. "A teasing flare for words." *–Village Voice.* "Unfailingly thought-provoking." *–LA Times.* "The play moves with the speed and logic of a dream." *–Seattle Weekly.* [2M] ISBN: 978-0-8222-2209-5

★ **THE INTELLIGENT DESIGN OF JENNY CHOW by Rolin Jones.** This irreverent "techno-comedy" chronicles one brilliant woman's quest to determine her heritage and face her fears with the help of her astounding creation called Jenny Chow. "Boldly imagined." *–NY Times.* "Fantastical and funny." *–Variety.* "Harvests many laughs and finally a few tears." *–LA Times.* [3M, 3W] ISBN: 978-0-8222-2071-8

★ **SOUVENIR by Stephen Temperley.** Florence Foster Jenkins, a wealthy society eccentric, suffers under the delusion that she is a great coloratura soprano—when in fact the opposite is true. "Hilarious and deeply touching. Incredibly moving and breathtaking." *–NY Daily News.* "A sweet love letter of a play." *–NY Times.* "Wildly funny. Completely charming." *–Star-Ledger.* [1M, 1W] ISBN: 978-0-8222-2157-9

★ **ICE GLEN by Joan Ackermann.** In this touching period comedy, a beautiful poetess dwells in idyllic obscurity on a Berkshire estate with a band of unlikely cohorts. "A beautifully written story of nature and change." *–Talkin' Broadway.* "A lovely play which will leave you with a lot to think about." *–CurtainUp.* "Funny, moving and witty." *–Metroland (Boston).* [4M, 3W] ISBN: 978-0-8222-2175-3

★ **THE LAST DAYS OF JUDAS ISCARIOT by Stephen Adly Guirgis.** Set in a time-bending, darkly comic world between heaven and hell, this play reexamines the plight and fate of the New Testament's most infamous sinner. "An unforced eloquence that finds the poetry in lowdown street talk." *–NY Times.* "A real jaw-dropper." *–Variety.* "An extraordinary play." *–Guardian (UK).* [10M, 5W] ISBN: 978-0-8222-2082-4

DRAMATISTS PLAY SERVICE, INC.
440 Park Avenue South, New York, NY 10016 212-683-8960 Fax 212-213-1539
postmaster@dramatists.com www.dramatists.com

NEW PLAYS

★ **THE GREAT AMERICAN TRAILER PARK MUSICAL music and lyrics by David Nehls, book by Betsy Kelso.** Pippi, a stripper on the run, has just moved into Armadillo Acres, wreaking havoc among the tenants of Florida's most exclusive trailer park. "Adultery, strippers, murderous ex-boyfriends, Costco and the Ice Capades. Undeniable fun." *–NY Post.* "Joyful and unashamedly vulgar." *–The New Yorker.* "Sparkles with treasure." *–New York Sun.* [2M, 5W] ISBN: 978-0-8222-2137-1

★ **MATCH by Stephen Belber.** When a young Seattle couple meet a prominent New York choreographer, they are led on a fraught journey that will change their lives forever. "Uproariously funny, deeply moving, enthralling theatre." *–NY Daily News.* "Prolific laughs and ear-to-ear smiles." *–NY Magazine.* [2M, 1W] ISBN: 978-0-8222-2020-6

★ **MR. MARMALADE by Noah Haidle.** Four-year-old Lucy's imaginary friend, Mr. Marmalade, doesn't have much time for her—not to mention he has a cocaine addiction and a penchant for pornography. "Alternately hilarious and heartbreaking." *–The New Yorker.* "A mature and accomplished play." *–LA Times.* "Scathingly observant comedy." *–Miami Herald.* [4M, 2W] ISBN: 978-0-8222-2142-5

★ **MOONLIGHT AND MAGNOLIAS by Ron Hutchinson.** Three men cloister themselves as they work tirelessly to reshape a screenplay that's just not working—*Gone with the Wind.* "Consumers of vintage Hollywood insider stories will eat up Hutchinson's diverting conjecture." *–Variety.* "A lot of fun." *–NY Post.* "A Hollywood dream-factory farce." *–Chicago Sun-Times.* [3M, 1W] ISBN: 978-0-8222-2084-8

★ **THE LEARNED LADIES OF PARK AVENUE by David Grimm, translated and freely adapted from Molière's *Les Femmes Savantes*.** Dicky wants to marry Betty, but her mother's plan is for Betty to wed a most pompous man. "A brave, brainy and barmy revision." *–Hartford Courant.* "A rare but welcome bird in contemporary theatre." *–New Haven Register.* "Roll over Cole Porter." *–Boston Globe.* [5M, 5W] ISBN: 978-0-8222-2135-7

★ **REGRETS ONLY by Paul Rudnick.** A sparkling comedy of Manhattan manners that explores the latest topics in marriage, friendships and squandered riches. "One of the funniest quip-meisters on the planet." *–NY Times.* "Precious moments of hilarity. Devastatingly accurate political and social satire." *–BackStage.* "Great fun." *–CurtainUp.* [3M, 3W] ISBN: 978-0-8222-2223-1

DRAMATISTS PLAY SERVICE, INC.
440 Park Avenue South, New York, NY 10016 212-683-8960 Fax 212-213-1539
postmaster@dramatists.com www.dramatists.com

NEW PLAYS

★ **AFTER ASHLEY by Gina Gionfriddo.** A teenager is unwillingly thrust into the national spotlight when a family tragedy becomes talk-show fodder. "A work that virtually any audience would find accessible." *–NY Times.* "Deft characterization and caustic humor." *–NY Sun.* "A smart satirical drama." *–Variety.* [4M, 2W] ISBN: 978-0-8222-2099-2

★ **THE RUBY SUNRISE by Rinne Groff.** Twenty-five years after Ruby struggles to realize her dream of inventing the first television, her daughter faces similar battles of faith as she works to get Ruby's story told on network TV. "Measured and intelligent, optimistic yet clear-eyed." *–NY Magazine.* "Maintains an exciting sense of ingenuity." *–Village Voice.* "Sinuous theatrical flair." *–Broadway.com.* [3M, 4W] ISBN: 978-0-8222-2140-1

★ **MY NAME IS RACHEL CORRIE taken from the writings of Rachel Corrie, edited by Alan Rickman and Katharine Viner.** This solo piece tells the story of Rachel Corrie who was killed in Gaza by an Israeli bulldozer set to demolish a Palestinian home. "Heartbreaking urgency. An invigoratingly detailed portrait of a passionate idealist." *–NY Times.* "Deeply authentically human." *–USA Today.* "A stunning dramatization." *–CurtainUp.* [1W] ISBN: 978-0-8222-2222-4

★ **ALMOST, MAINE by John Cariani.** A cast of Mainers (or "Mainiacs" if you prefer) fall in and out of love in ways that only people who live in close proximity to wild moose can do. "A whimsical approach to the joys and perils of romance." *–NY Times.* "Sweet, poignant and witty." *–NY Daily News.* "John Cariani aims for the heart by way of the funny bone." *–Star-Ledger.* [2M, 2W] ISBN: 978-0-8222-2156-2

★ **Mitch Albom's TUESDAYS WITH MORRIE by Jeffrey Hatcher and Mitch Albom, based on the book by Mitch Albom.** The true story of Brandeis University professor Morrie Schwartz and his relationship with his student Mitch Albom. "A touching, life-affirming, deeply emotional drama." *–NY Daily News.* "You'll laugh. You'll cry." *–Variety.* "Moving and powerful." *–NY Post.* [2M] ISBN: 978-0-8222-2188-3

★ **DOG SEES GOD: CONFESSIONS OF A TEENAGE BLOCKHEAD by Bert V. Royal.** An abused pianist and a pyromaniac ex-girlfriend contribute to the teen-angst of America's most hapless kid. "A welcome antidote to the notion that the *Peanuts* gang provides merely American cuteness." *–NY Times.* "Hysterically funny." *–NY Post.* "The *Peanuts* kids have finally come out of their shells." *–Time Out.* [4M, 4W] ISBN: 978-0-8222-2152-4

DRAMATISTS PLAY SERVICE, INC.
440 Park Avenue South, New York, NY 10016 212-683-8960 Fax 212-213-1539
postmaster@dramatists.com www.dramatists.com

NEW PLAYS

★ **RABBIT HOLE by David Lindsay-Abaire.** Winner of the 2007 Pulitzer Prize. Becca and Howie Corbett have everything a couple could want until a life-shattering accident turns their world upside down. "An intensely emotional examination of grief, laced with wit." *–Variety.* "A transcendent and deeply affecting new play." *–Entertainment Weekly.* "Painstakingly beautiful." *–BackStage.* [2M, 3W] ISBN: 978-0-8222-2154-8

★ **DOUBT, A Parable by John Patrick Shanley.** Winner of the 2005 Pulitzer Prize and Tony Award. Sister Aloysius, a Bronx school principal, takes matters into her own hands when she suspects the young Father Flynn of improper relations with one of the male students. "All the elements come invigoratingly together like clockwork." *–Variety.* "Passionate, exquisite, important, engrossing." *–NY Newsday.* [1M, 3W] ISBN: 978-0-8222-2219-4

★ **THE PILLOWMAN by Martin McDonagh.** In an unnamed totalitarian state, an author of horrific children's stories discovers that someone has been making his stories come true. "A blindingly bright black comedy." *–NY Times.* "McDonagh's least forgiving, bravest play." *–Variety.* "Thoroughly startling and genuinely intimidating." *–Chicago Tribune.* [4M, 5 bit parts (2M, 1W, 1 boy, 1 girl)] ISBN: 978-0-8222-2100-5

★ **GREY GARDENS book by Doug Wright, music by Scott Frankel, lyrics by Michael Korie.** The hilarious and heartbreaking story of Big Edie and Little Edie Bouvier Beale, the eccentric aunt and cousin of Jacqueline Kennedy Onassis, once bright names on the social register who became East Hampton's most notorious recluses. "An experience no passionate theatergoer should miss." *–NY Times.* "A unique and unmissable musical." *–Rolling Stone.* [4M, 3W, 2 girls] ISBN: 978-0-8222-2181-4

★ **THE LITTLE DOG LAUGHED by Douglas Carter Beane.** Mitchell Green could make it big as the hot new leading man in Hollywood if Diane, his agent, could just keep him in the closet. "Devastatingly funny." *–NY Times.* "An out-and-out delight." *–NY Daily News.* "Full of wit and wisdom." *–NY Post.* [2M, 2W] ISBN: 978-0-8222-2226-2

★ **SHINING CITY by Conor McPherson.** A guilt-ridden man reaches out to a therapist after seeing the ghost of his recently deceased wife. "Haunting, inspired and glorious." *–NY Times.* "Simply breathtaking and astonishing." *–Time Out.* "A thoughtful, artful, absorbing new drama." *–Star-Ledger.* [3M, 1W] ISBN: 978-0-8222-2187-6

DRAMATISTS PLAY SERVICE, INC.
440 Park Avenue South, New York, NY 10016 212-683-8960 Fax 212-213-1539
postmaster@dramatists.com www.dramatists.com